George Washington at Logstown

by Sophie Panella and Kylee Chamberlain
with Brenda Applegate

Dedicated to the Native Americans who once made this region their home.

Text by Sophie Panella and Kylee Chamberlain with Brenda Applegate of the Beaver County Historical Research & Landmarks Foundation with assistance from the following:
   Patrick Riley (Legion Ville Historical Society, Sewickley, Pennsylvania),
   Marilyn Black (Vice President for Heritage Development Oil Region Alliance of Business, Industry & Tourism),

Proofreading by Taylor Breaden and Carrie Zuberbuhler Kennedy, M. Ed.

Cover art by Marilyn Freeman and Deborah Brimner, using a photograph of the Logstown Diorama by Patrick Riley, a portrait of George Washington by Portrait by Charles Wilson Peale, c. 1772. Washington-Custis-Lee Collection (at Washington and Lee University) in Lexington, Virginia and of Tanacharison by Robert Griffing.

Painting of canoes and tree and Tanacharison by Robert Griffing
Painting of Washington's meeting at Logstown by Andrew Knez
Drawing of Fort Le Boeuf from the Fort LeBoeuf Historical Society
Painting of Washington at the Point 1753, Washington and Gist on the River by John Buxton
Old Town Alexandria Farmers Market by Patricia Palermino
Painting of General Anthony Wayne's cantonment at Legion Ville (1792-1793) by James Petrosky of Harmony Township, Pa.

Photos of people reading Washington's Journal in Alexandria Square were taken at the 2018 STEM Family Night at Baden Academy. How many can you find?

Copyright © 2019 by Grow a Generation Sewickley, PA 15143 **growageneration.com**

All rights reserved. This book or any portion thereof may not be reproduced or used in any manner whatsoever without the express written permission of the publisher except for the use of brief quotations in a book review or scholarly journal.

ISBN 978-1-79477-101-7

Any and all profit from the sale of this book benefit Beaver County Historical Research & Landmarks Foundation.

> Sophie, I had no idea that there was an Indian Village here in Baden!

> Let's find out more!

LOGSTOWN

One of the large Indian towns on the upper Ohio was located nearby in 1727-58. Important conferences were held here between the British, French, and Indians in the struggle for the Ohio country.

PENNSYLVANIA HISTORICAL AND MUSEUM COMMISSION

Sophie and Kylee found a historical marker in Baden, Pennsylvania!

Check out this diorama of Logstown at the Captain William Vicary Mansion in Beaver County. It's amazing to imagine a large Native American settlement along the Ohio River. Logstown got its name from logs piled up on a large sandbar at the village after storms.

The Ohio River must have been so different back in the 1700s. There were Indians here, as well as French and British. The American Revolution hadn't happened yet, but many of the people who would fight for freedom were some of the traders and soldiers working with the Indians.

The artist who created this image of Logstown referred to a journal from a priest visiting the area four years before Washington's visit. Father Bonnescamps described "dining in a hollow cotton wood" that fit 29 people! We call this type of tree today a sycamore.

George Washington came to Logstown when he was 21 years old. He held council with Tanacharison, Scaroudy (also named Monacatootha), Shingas, and other Indian chiefs in November of 1753 while on his important mission to Fort Le Boeuf.

Washington was on a mission from the British Governor of the Colony of Virginia. He was commissioned by Governor Robert Dinwiddie of Virginia to deliver the Governor's message to St. Pierre, commandant of the French forts on the Ohio River. The letter said that the French were intruding on English territory.

This is a portrait of Major Washington in 1753, and he is wearing the uniform of a British provincial soldier. Remember, this was 23 years BEFORE the Declaration of Independence and the American Revolution. This portrait was painted by Charles Willson Peale of Washington as a colonel during the French and Indian War. He looks so young!

Washington left Virginia and traveled to Maryland to meet up with the Ohio Company's representative Christopher Gist and Jacob Van Braam. They traveled on horseback, foot, and canoe across the Appalachian Mountains all the way to the Ohio River and the town of Logstown.

You could find Indians from many tribes in Logstown, including the Delaware, Shawnee, Seneca, Wyandot, Mohawk, and Miami, as welll as some members of the Six Nations who were known to be Mingoes.

Washington went to meet the Iroquois Half King Tanacharison at Logstown. The chief was at his hunting camp, fifteen miles away on the Little Beaver. Runners had to go and ask Tanacharison to return to Logstown.

When first meeting Washington, Tanacharison said he knew who Washington was, "You are Conotocarious," he said, which meant "devourer of villages." The nickname had previously been given to Washington's great-grandfather, John Washington, in the late seventeenth century. I think Major Washington would have wanted to appear fierce in the company of the Indians.

Washington asked their help to travel to the French forts north of Logstown. He wanted to find the French commander to deliver the Governor's message. It must have been so hard to travel when there were no roads and no street signs.

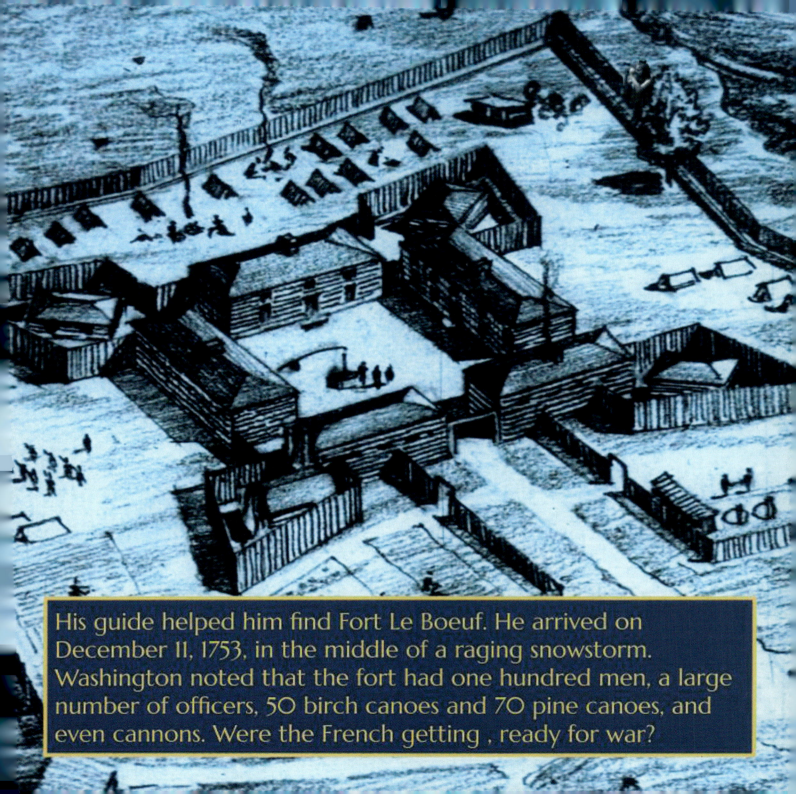

His guide helped him find Fort Le Boeuf. He arrived on December 11, 1753, in the middle of a raging snowstorm. Washington noted that the fort had one hundred men, a large number of officers, 50 birch canoes and 70 pine canoes, and even cannons. Were the French getting, ready for war?

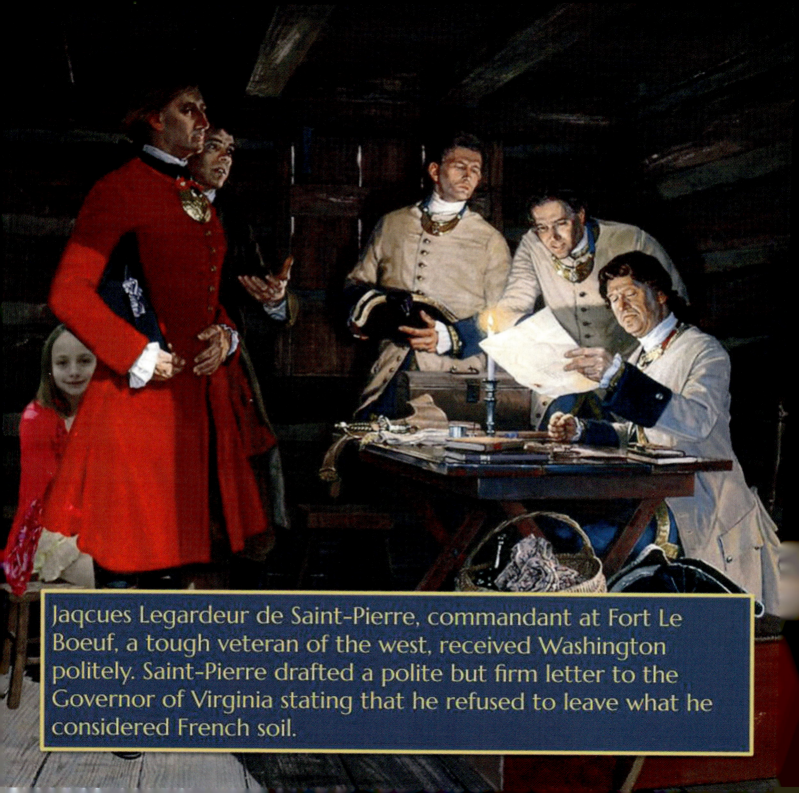

Jaqcues Legardeur de Saint-Pierre, commandant at Fort Le Boeuf, a tough veteran of the west, received Washington politely. Saint-Pierre drafted a polite but firm letter to the Governor of Virginia stating that he refused to leave what he considered French soil.

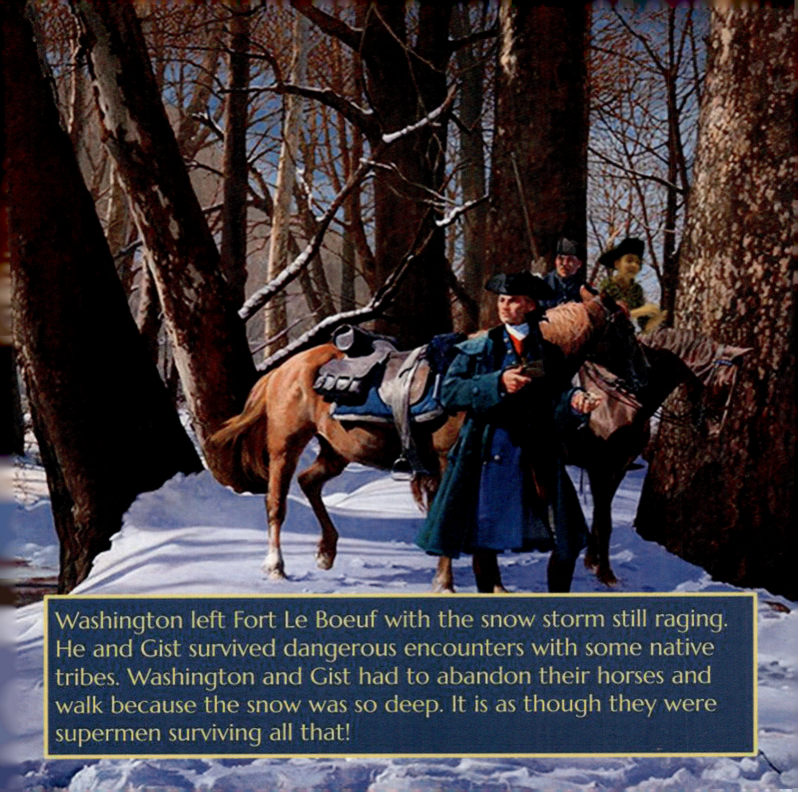

Washington left Fort Le Boeuf with the snow storm still raging. He and Gist survived dangerous encounters with some native tribes. Washington and Gist had to abandon their horses and walk because the snow was so deep. It is as though they were supermen surviving all that!

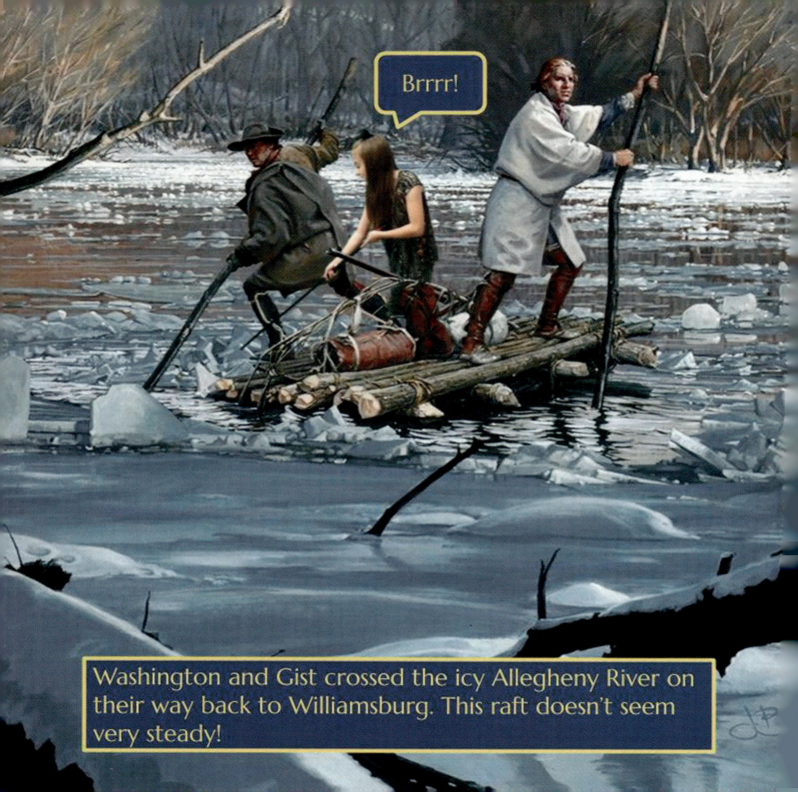

Washington and Gist crossed the icy Allegheny River on their way back to Williamsburg. This raft doesn't seem very steady!

While trying to cross the river near what is now Pittsburgh, Washington was knocked overboard by a river flowing with ice. Gist pulled him onto the raft and made for an island in the middle of the river. They spent the night on the island trying to dry out. They were so wet they couldn't start a fire. In the morning they found their luck had changed. The river had frozen solid in the cold. Washington and Gist walked to the shore and proceeded as quickly as possible all the way back to Williamsburg.

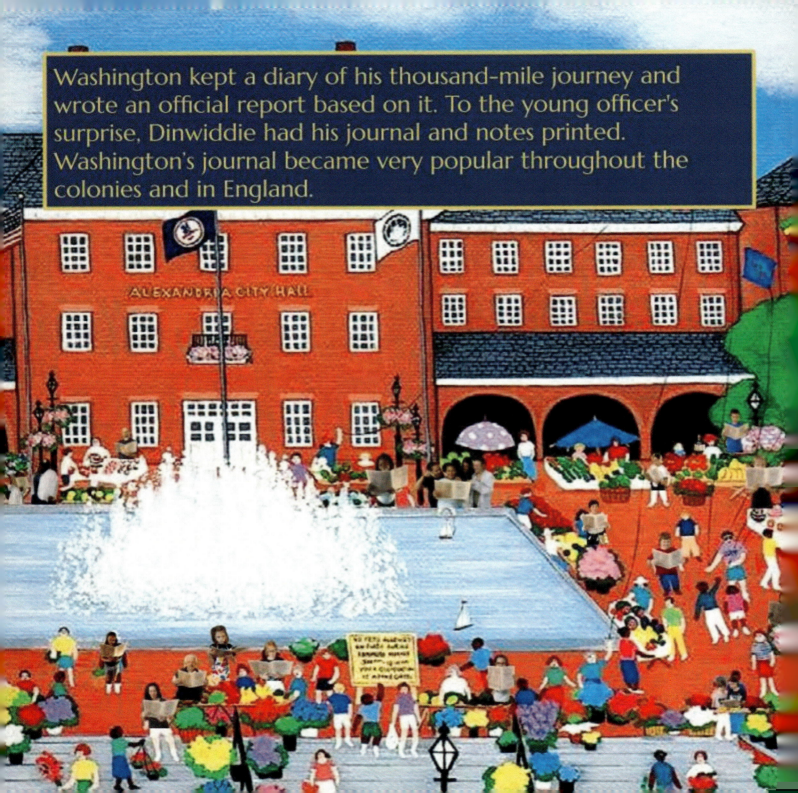

Washington kept a diary of his thousand-mile journey and wrote an official report based on it. To the young officer's surprise, Dinwiddie had his journal and notes printed. Washington's journal became very popular throughout the colonies and in England.

George Washington went on to live an extraordinary life. He fought in the French and Indian War and was made the Commander-in-Chief of the Continental Army. He was so respected and loved, Congress made him the first president of the United States.

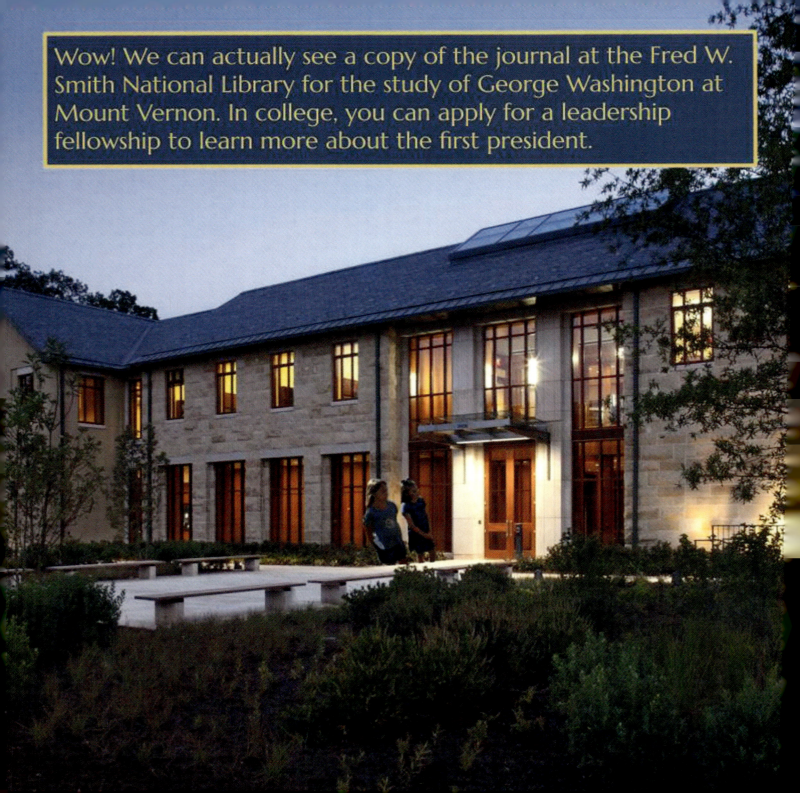

Wow! We can actually see a copy of the journal at the Fred W. Smith National Library for the study of George Washington at Mount Vernon. In college, you can apply for a leadership fellowship to learn more about the first president.

There is a famous statue atop Mt. Washington in Pittsburgh that shows George Washington deep in conversation with the Seneca leader Guyasuta. Guyasuta was one of his guides on the trip to Fort Le Beouf. The sculpture commemorates a meeting in 1770. The two sat for hours in discussion over who could live on the lands that would become Pittsburgh.

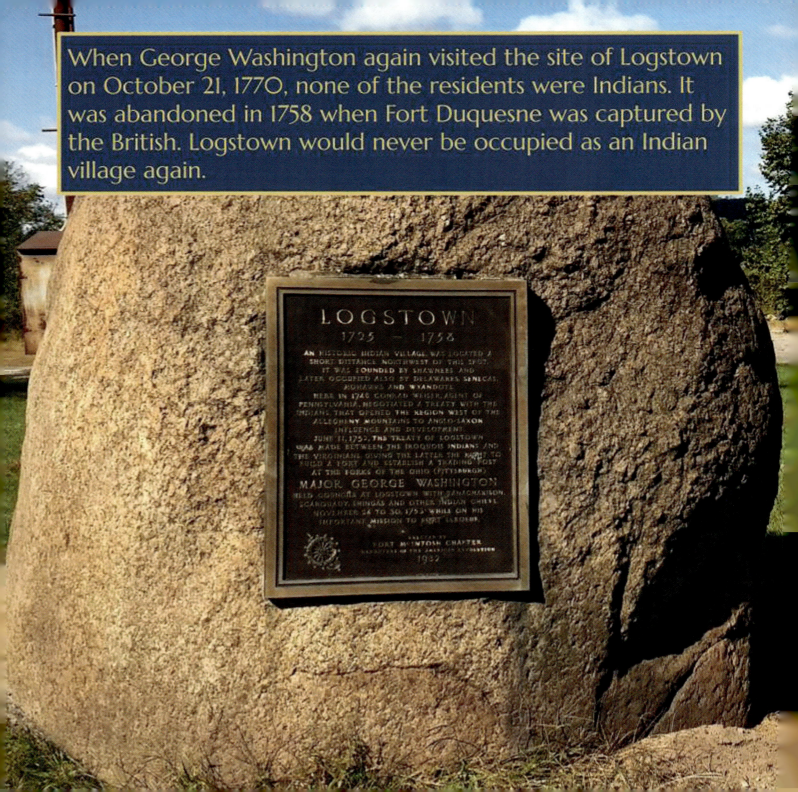

When George Washington again visited the site of Logstown on October 21, 1770, none of the residents were Indians. It was abandoned in 1758 when Fort Duquesne was captured by the British. Logstown would never be occupied as an Indian village again.

What happened to Logstown?

- In 1758, French and English armies forced Indians to abandon Logstown and the area.
- In 1770, George Washington visited Logstown one last time. None of the residents were Indians.
- In 1792, Major General Anthony Wayne came to this area which he named Legion Ville. This was the General's headquarters from 1792-1793,.
- In 1803, Meriwether Lewis' boat got stuck on the Logstown Sandbar and had to be pulled off by a team of oxen.
- In 1824, the Harmony Society purchased 3,000 acres of ground and built Economy Village on the land. You can visit parts of Old Economy today.
- In 1838, Baden was founded.

Logstown Today

There are several monuments and signs commemorating Logstown and its history as Legion Ville. They are in Baden collected on a plot of land along Duss Avenue. We were able to visit but were sad that it was not safe enough to bring our class. We invite you to work with the Beaver County Historical Research and Landmarks Foundation to reclaim and renovate the site for classroom and community visits.

Above is a picture of the Logstown site before stores and roads became established. To the right are two pictures of the site today taken from the edge of Duss Avenue near the intersection of Legionville Road.

What happened to the Indians?

Logstown was founded by Chief Kakowatchiky, a Shawnee Indian. There are 7,500 Shawnee Indians today mostly in Oklahoma.

Tanacharison was originally from the Catawba tribe. There are 3,370 living Catawbas mostly in South Carolina.

Tanacharison was adopted by the Seneca tribe after he was taken captive by the French. The Seneca tribe was one of the Six Nations of the Iroquois Confederacy. There are 125,000 in Canada and the United States. They prefer the name Haudenosaunee, which means People of the Longhouse. They include Seneca, Oneida, Mohawk, Cayuga, Tuscaroras, and Onondaga.

Thanks to the Washington's Trail 1753, you can find signs that point out the way George Washington traveled during this mission. WASHINGTON'S TRAIL is a driving route through western Pennsylvania. Traversing modern highways, the route commemorates young Washington's first military and diplomatic venture in the Fall and Winter of 1753 - 1754. You can visit their website at www.washintongstrail.org to download the map and find other resources.

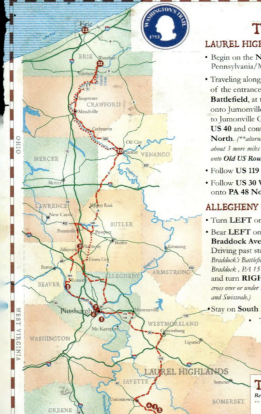

WASHINGTON'S NORTHERN TREK THROUGH WESTERN PENNSYLVANIA

LAUREL HIGHLANDS
- Begin on the **National Rd.**, **US 40 West** at the Pennsylvania/Maryland border.
- Traveling along US 40, approximately five miles west of the entrance gate to **Fort Necessity National Battlefield**, at the crest of the Summit, turn right onto **Jumonville Rd.** Follow approximately 3 miles to Jumonville Glen and Dunbar's Camp. Return to **US 40** and continue west to Uniontown to **US 119 North**. *(**alternate route**: Passing Dunbar's Camp, continue about 3 more miles to the foot of the mountain. Turn **RIGHT** onto **Old US Route 119** and follow to **US 119 North**.)*
- Follow **US 119 N** to **US 30 West**.
- Follow **US 30 West** (Lincoln Highway.) Turn **RIGHT** onto **PA 48 North** and follow 2.5 miles.

ALLEGHENY COUNTY
- Turn **LEFT** onto **PA 130 West**, follow 3.8 miles.
- Bear **LEFT** onto **Tri-Boro Ave.**, which becomes **Braddock Ave.** and then **S. Braddock Ave.** Driving past steel mills and through Braddock *(note: Braddock's Battlefield History Center is located at 609 6th St., Braddock, PA 15104)*, turn **RIGHT** (just before bridge) and **RIGHT** again at the stop sign. *(note: do not cross over or under Rankin Bridge. Follow signs for Pittsburgh and Swissvale.)*
- Stay on **South Braddock Ave.** for several miles.
- Turn **LEFT** onto **Penn Ave.** (PA 8) and follow through East Liberty and continue to **Downtown Pittsburgh**. At Point State Park in Downtown Pittsburgh, turn
- **LEFT** onto **Commonwealth Place**. *(note: Fort Pitt Museum is located in Point State Park.)*
- Follow signs for **Fort Duquesne Bridge** and after crossing bridge exit onto **PA 65 North**.
- Follow **PA 65 North** (Ohio River Boulevard) about 15 miles.

BEAVER COUNTY
- Turn **RIGHT** onto **Conway-Wallrose Rd.** (13th Street/PA 2008.)
- Turn onto **PA 989 North**.

BUTLER COUNTY
- Turn **RIGHT** onto **PA 68 East** through Zelienople to Harmony on the left.
- Take **Main St.** in Harmony, turn **RIGHT** onto **Mercer Rd.** Follow **Mercer Rd.** to **US 19 North**.
- Follow **US 19 North** to Portersville.
- Take **West Park Rd.** north to **US 422 East**.
- Follow **US 422 East** to **PA 528 North**.
- Take **PA 528 North** to **PA 8** and **PA 173 North**.
- Take **PA 173 North** to Slippery Rock and **PA 108 East**.
- Follow **PA 108 East** to **PA 8 North**.

VENANGO/MERCER COUNTIES
- Near Wesley, take **Old Route 8** to Franklin.
- From Franklin, follow **US 322 West** to Meadville.

CRAWFORD COUNTY
- In Meadville, turn **LEFT** onto **Linden St.**
- At the second traffic light, turn **RIGHT** onto **US 6/19 French Creek Parkway**.
- At end of **Parkway** (approx. 3 miles) turn **LEFT** following **US 6/19 North** through Saegertown.
- Venango – turn **RIGHT** to stay on **US 6/19**.
- Cambridge Springs – turn **LEFT** to stay on **US 6/19**.

ERIE COUNTY
- Follow **US 19 North** to **Fort LeBoeuf Museum** in Waterford.

WASHINGTON'S RETURN ROUTE

Return from Erie County on the same route into Cambridge Springs. *(note: Washington traveled back from the French fort by canoe via French Creek.)*

CRAWFORD COUNTY
- In Cambridge Springs, follow **PA 86/S. Main St.**
- In Meadville, follow **PA 86/N. Main St.** to **S. Main St.** to **US 322 East**.
- Reverse northern route through Mercer and Venango Counties.

BUTLER COUNTY
- Continue south on **PA 8** to the Old Stone House.
- Turn **RIGHT** onto **PA 528**. Follow to Prospect and Evans City. *(note: To see George Washington monument, take PA 68 East, then return to Evans City.)*
- Turn **RIGHT PA 68 WEST**, immediately after railroad tracks, take **Franklin Rd.**, which splits off to the left.

ALLEGHENY COUNTY
- Follow **Franklin Rd.** to **Bakerstown/Warrendale Rd.** (Red Belt) and turn **RIGHT**.
- Follow **Red Belt** about one mile and turn **LEFT** onto **US 19 South**. Follow 1.8 miles, turn **LEFT** onto **N. Chapel Road**. Turn **LEFT** onto **PA 910** (Orange Belt), follow 6.5 miles.
- Turn **LEFT** onto **PA 8 South**, follow 10 miles.
- Merge onto **PA 28 South**.
- Follow **PA 28** to the 40th Street Bridge at Washington Crossing.
- Turn **LEFT** and cross the bridge and continue straight at end of bridge.
- Turn **LEFT** onto **Penn Ave.** *(note: Penn Ave. becomes PA 8 and US 30.)*
- Follow **US 30 East/Lincoln Hwy.** through Irwin to Greensburg.

LAUREL HIGHLANDS
- Take **US 119 South** in Greensburg, towards Connellsville and Uniontown.
- In Uniontown, take **US 40 East/National Rd.**
- Follow **US 40** across the PA and MD border.

THE TRAIL
Return trail deviates from Northern Route
** Numbers on map correspond to points of interest found throughout the brochure.
** There may be areas of the route without signage.

Beaver County Historical Research and Landmarks Foundation

Welcome to the Home of the BCHR&LF!

Parlor | Captain William Vicary Mansion | Bake Oven

Any profits from the sale of this book are directed to the Beaver County Historical Research and Landmarks Foundation. The Foundation exists to research, collect and archive local history and artifacts, recognize Beaver County landmarks and educate the local and national audience via instructional programs, reference materials, publications, referrals and special events.

Brenda Applegate
Director, BCHRLF
Beaver County Historical Research and Landmarks Foundation

Special thanks to our mentor Brenda Applegate and to Patrick Riley of the Legion Ville Historical Society. Their dedicat to preserving local history and supporting community organizations is safeguarding history for current and future generations.

A re-creation of the late 18th century training site Legion Ville, established by Major General "Mad" Anthony Wayne on the site that once was Logstown.

Patrick Riley
Archaeologist/Historian
President, Legion Ville Historical Society

Sophie, there's another sign here!

Baden Academy Charter School

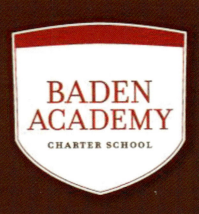

This public charter school in Western PA works to inspire personal excellence. They cultivate the inherent gifts and talents present in all children by providing a curriculum that integrates the arts and sciences in a highly interactive, hands-on environment.

Grow a Generation

Grow a Generation partners with gifted and talented young people and teachers to make meaningful projects possible. Faculty, students, and student teams apply in their school to be accepted into the fellowship program. Once selected, they embark on a year-long odyssey to publish a book, create a digital artifact, or enter a STEM competition. Find out more at growageneration.com